Section One — Rivers

Section One — Rivers

Page 3 — The Hydrological Cycle

1 (a) (i) A — evaporation *[1 mark]*.
B — transpiration *[1 mark]*.
(ii) Evaporation is when water is heated by the sun and turns into water vapour *[1 mark]*. Transpiration is the evaporation of water from plants *[1 mark]*.
(b) It's moved inland by winds *[1 mark]*. The water vapour then condenses to form clouds *[1 mark]* and falls onto the land as precipitation *[1 mark]*.
(c) Channel storage *[1 mark]* is when water is held in a river *[1 mark]*. / Interception storage *[1 mark]* is when water lands on things like plant leaves and doesn't hit the ground *[1 mark]*. / Surface storage *[1 mark]* is when water is held in things like lakes/reservoirs/puddles *[1 mark]*.
(d) (i) Infiltration *[1 mark]*
(ii) The water could flow to the sea by throughflow *[1 mark]*. This is when water in the soil flows downhill *[1 mark]*. The water could also percolate into the rock and end up in the sea by groundwater flow *[1 mark]*. This is when water in rock flows downhill *[1 mark]*.

Page 4 — Drainage Basins

1 (a) (i) One mark for both labels correct.

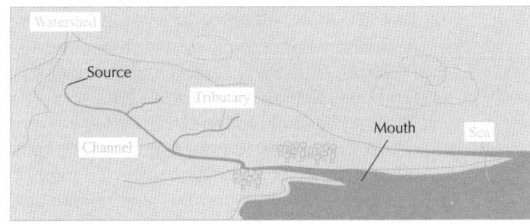

(ii) A confluence *[1 mark]*
(iii) It's a smaller river that joins a main river *[1 mark]*.
(iv) It's a ridge of high land that separates two drainage basins *[1 mark]*. Water falling either side of the ridge will go into different drainage basins *[1 mark]*.
(b) They are open systems *[1 mark]* because there are inputs of water to them and outputs of water from them *[1 mark]*.
(c) One mark for each correct flow and output.

INPUTS	FLOWS	STORES	OUTPUTS
Precipitation	Channel flow	Channel storage	River flow into the sea
	Infiltration	Groundwater storage	Evaporation
	Throughflow	Interception storage	Transpiration
	Percolation	Surface storage	
	Groundwater flow		
	Surface runoff		

Page 5 — Weathering and the River Valley

1 (a) Water gets into rock that has cracks, e.g. granite *[1 mark]*. The water freezes at night and expands, which puts pressure on the rock *[1 mark]*. The water then thaws during the day and contracts, which releases the pressure on the rock *[1 mark]*. Repeated freezing and thawing widens the cracks and causes the rock to break up *[1 mark]*.
(b) Chemical weathering is the breakdown of rocks by changing their chemical composition *[1 mark]*. Mechanical weathering is the breakdown of rocks by physical processes, without changing their chemical composition *[1 mark]*.
(c) Biological weathering is the breakdown of rocks by living things, e.g. plant roots break down rocks by growing into cracks and pushing them apart *[1 mark]*.

2 (a) One mark for both labels correct.

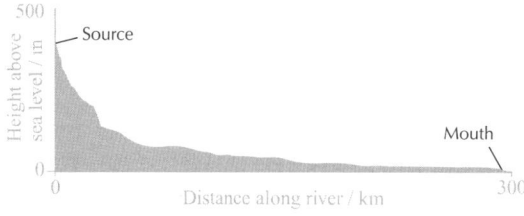

(b) (i) The long profile shows how the gradient (steepness) of a river changes along its length *[1 mark]*. The cross profile shows what a cross section of a river looks like at a specific point *[1 mark]*.
(ii) Cross profile at point A — a V-shaped valley with steep sides *[1 mark]* and a narrow, shallow channel *[1 mark]*.
Cross profile at point B — a valley with gently sloping sides *[1 mark]* and a wider, deeper channel than at point A *[1 mark]*.

Page 6 — Erosion, Transportation and Deposition

1 (a) (i) 10 km *[1 mark]*
(ii) The river's velocity is 0.8 m per second *[1 mark]*. Pebbles are transported by saltation *[1 mark]*.
(iii) Traction *[1 mark]* is when large particles are pushed along the river bed by the force of the water *[1 mark]*. / Suspension *[1 mark]* is when small particles are carried along by the water *[1 mark]*. / Solution *[1 mark]* is when soluble materials are dissolved in the water and carried along *[1 mark]*.
(b) Hydraulic action — the force of the water breaks rock particles away from the river channel *[1 mark]*.
Corrasion — eroded rocks picked up by the river scrape and rub against the channel, wearing it away *[1 mark]*.
Attrition — eroded rocks picked up by the river smash into each other and break into smaller, more rounded fragments *[1 mark]*.
Corrosion — river water dissolves some types of rock, e.g. chalk and limestone *[1 mark]*.
(c) E.g. rivers slow down when the volume of water in the river falls *[1 mark]*. They also slow down when the amount of eroded material in the water increases *[1 mark]*, when the water is shallower, e.g. on the inside of a bend *[1 mark]*, and when they reach their mouth *[1 mark]*.

Page 7 — Erosional River Landforms

1 (a) The map shows waterfalls, which are found in the upper course of a river *[1 mark]*. The land around the Afon Merch is high (around 500 m in grid square 6353) *[1 mark]*. The river crosses lots of contours lines in a short distance, which means it's steep *[1 mark]*. The river is narrow (shown on the map by a thin line) *[1 mark]*.
(b) (i) 633525 (accept 634524) *[1 mark]*
(ii) Waterfalls form where a river flows over an area of hard rock followed by an area of softer rock *[1 mark]*. The softer rock is eroded more than the hard rock, creating a step in the river *[1 mark]*. As water goes over the step it erodes more and more of the softer rock *[1 mark]*. A steep drop is eventually created, which is called a waterfall *[1 mark]*.

Section One — Rivers

2   This question is level marked. There are also 3 extra marks available for spelling, punctuation and grammar. HINTS:
   - Make sure your spelling, punctuation and grammar is *consistently correct*, that your meaning is *clear* and that you use a range of geographical terms *correctly*.
   - Start by introducing the *river* you've decided to write about by saying *where it is* and a few *facts* about it, e.g. 'The River Clyde flows north-west through Scotland, from the Southern Uplands to the west coast. The River Clyde is about 160 km long'.
   - Then *describe* the *location* of an *erosional landform* on the river and *explain how it formed*, e.g. 'There are interlocking spurs at Crawford. The spurs are between 300 and 500 m high. Most of the erosion in the upper course of the River Clyde is vertically downwards, which has created steep-sided V-shaped valleys. It's not powerful enough to erode laterally so it has to wind around the high hillsides that stick out into its path on either side. This has formed the interlocking spurs'.
   - Then describe the location of *another* erosional landform on the river, e.g. a waterfall or a gorge, and *explain* how it formed.

Page 8 — Erosional and Depositional River Landforms

1 (a) (i)   A river cliff is likely to be found at A *[1 mark]*. The current is faster on the outside bend of the meander because the channel is deeper *[1 mark]*. This means there's more erosion on the outside bend, so a river cliff is formed *[1 mark]*.
   (ii)   A slip-off slope is likely to be found at B *[1 mark]*. The current is slower on the inside bend of the meander because the river channel is shallower *[1 mark]*. This means material is deposited on the inside of the bend, so a slip-off slope is formed *[1 mark]*.
(b) (i)   The neck of the meander *[1 mark]*.
   (ii)   Erosion causes the outside bends of a meander to get closer *[1 mark]* until there's only a small area of land left between the bends (called a neck) *[1 mark]*. The river breaks through this land, for example during a flood *[1 mark]*. The river then flows along the shortest course *[1 mark]*. Deposition eventually cuts off the meander *[1 mark]* so an ox-bow lake is formed *[1 mark]*.

Page 9 — Depositional River Landforms

1 (a) (i)   One mark for correct labelling.

   Flood plain

   (ii)   The wide valley floor on either side of a river which occasionally gets flooded *[1 mark]*.
   (iii)   When a river floods onto a flood plain the water slows down *[1 mark]* and deposits the eroded material it's transporting, which builds up the flood plain *[1 mark]*. Flood plains are also built up by the deposition that happens on the slip-off slopes of meanders *[1 mark]*.

(b) (i)   Natural embankments along the edges of a river channel *[1 mark]*.
   (ii)   When a river floods the heaviest material is deposited closest to the river channel because it gets dropped first when the river slows down *[1 mark]*. Over time, the deposited material builds up, creating levees along the edges of the river channel *[1 mark]*.
2 (a)   Cuspate delta *[1 mark]*.
(b)   Rivers are forced to slow down when they meet the sea or a lake. This causes them to deposit the material that they're carrying *[1 mark]*. If the sea doesn't wash away the material it builds up and the channel gets blocked *[1 mark]*. This forces the channel to split up into lots of smaller rivers called distributaries *[1 mark]*. Eventually the material builds up so much that low-lying areas of land called deltas are formed *[1 mark]*.

Pages 10-11 — The Storm Hydrograph

1 (a) (i)   Peak discharge — the highest discharge in the period of time you are looking at *[1 mark]*.
   Lag time — the delay between peak rainfall and peak discharge *[1 mark]*.
   (ii)   20:00 on day 1 *[1 mark]*.
   (iii)   18 hours *[1 mark]*.
(b) (i)   The hydrograph for the River Seeton has much steeper rising and falling limbs than the hydrograph for the River Dorth *[1 mark]*. / The peak discharge of the River Seeton (around 45 cumecs) was much higher than the peak discharge of the River Dorth (around 17 cumecs) *[1 mark]*. / The River Seeton had a shorter lag time (16 hours) than the River Dorth (18 hours) *[1 mark]*. / The peak rainfall around the River Seeton was much higher (just under 40 mm) than the peak rainfall around the River Dorth (just under 20 mm) *[1 mark]*.
   (ii)   E.g. there was about 20 mm more rainfall around the River Seeton than around the River Dorth *[1 mark]*. This would have caused more runoff into the river channel, so a higher discharge and a shorter lag time *[1 mark]*. / The rainfall around the River Seeton may have been more intense than around the River Dorth *[1 mark]*. This would have caused more runoff into the river channel, so a higher discharge and a shorter lag time *[1 mark]*. / There may be more urban areas around the River Seeton than the River Dorth which are covered with impermeable materials like concrete *[1 mark]*. This increases runoff into the river channel, which increases discharge and shortens the lag time *[1 mark]*.
2 (a) (i)   The rising limb would be steeper *[1 mark]*, there would be a shorter lag time *[1 mark]* and a larger peak discharge *[1 mark]*.
   (ii)   Over the 40 year period, the amount of woodland/ rural land has decreased *[1 mark]*. This means there's less vegetation to intercept rainfall and fewer roots to slow down throughflow *[1 mark]*. More water reaches the channel in a shorter amount of time, increasing the peak discharge, reducing the lag time and giving a steeper rising limb *[1 mark]*. The number and size of urban areas increased between 1960 and 2000 *[1 mark]*. Urban areas have drainage systems and they're covered with impermeable materials *[1 mark]*. More water reaches the channel in a shorter amount of time, increasing the peak discharge, reducing the lag time and giving a steeper rising limb *[1 mark]*.
(b) (i)   It happens because most rainwater doesn't land directly in the river channel *[1 mark]*. There's a delay as rainwater gets to the channel by flowing quickly overland or slowly underground *[1 mark]*.

CGP

GCSE
Geography
OCR B Specification

Answer Book
Higher Level

Contents

Section One — Rivers *3*

Section Two — Coasts *5*

Section Three — Population *7*

Section Four — Settlement *10*

Section Five — Tectonic Hazards *12*

Section Six — Climatic Hazards *14*

Section Seven — Development *16*

Section Eight — Industry *17*

Section Nine — Globalisation *20*

Published by CGP

ISBN: 978 1 84762 375 1
www.cgpbooks.co.uk
Printed by Elanders Ltd, Newcastle upon Tyne.
Clipart from Corel®

Based on the classic CGP style created by Richard Parsons.

Text, design, layout and original illustrations © Coordination Group Publications Ltd. (CGP) 2010
All rights reserved.

Section Two — Coasts

(ii) More runoff occurs on steep slopes, so there's a shorter lag time *[1 mark]*. Previously wet conditions mean water can't infiltrate the soil. This means there's more runoff and a shorter lag time *[1 mark]*.

Page 12 — Flooding — Causes

1 (a) (i) The frequency of flooding of the River Turb has increased between 1997 and 2008 *[1 mark]*, e.g. between 1997 and 2002 there were two floods, but between 2002 and 2008 there were 16 floods *[1 mark]*.

(ii) The River Turb may flood because of prolonged rainfall *[1 mark]*. After a long period of rainfall the soil becomes saturated so any further rainfall can't infiltrate. Runoff is increased, so discharge will increase quickly and cause a flood *[1 mark]*. / The River Turb may flood because of heavy rainfall *[1 mark]*. Heavy rainfall means runoff is increased, so discharge will increase quickly and cause a flood *[1 mark]*. / The River Turb may flood because of higher than normal snowmelt *[1 mark]*. When snow and ice melts, a lot of water goes into the river in a short space of time. This means discharge will increase quickly and cause a flood *[1 mark]*.

(b) The risk of flooding would be lower *[1 mark]* because more water percolates into the rock instead of flowing on the surface *[1 mark]*. This means there's less runoff and a longer lag time, so peak discharge will be lower *[1 mark]*.

(c) E.g. trees intercept rainwater on their leaves, which then evaporates, and they also take up water from the ground and store it *[1 mark]*. Deforestation increases the volume of water that reaches the river channel because less is intercepted and taken up from the ground by trees *[1 mark]*. This increases discharge and makes flooding more likely *[1 mark]*. Urban areas have lots of buildings and roads made from impermeable materials *[1 mark]*. Impermeable surfaces increase runoff and drains quickly take runoff to rivers *[1 mark]*. This means urbanisation can increase river discharge and so increase the risk of flooding *[1 mark]*.

Page 13 — Flood Management

1 (a) Hard engineering strategies use man-made structures to control the flow of rivers and reduce flooding *[1 mark]*. Soft engineering strategies are schemes set up using knowledge of a river and its processes to reduce the effects of flooding *[1 mark]*.

(b) (i) Channel straightening has been used to protect Moritt *[1 mark]*. This may cause flooding or increased erosion at Fultow because flood water is carried there faster *[1 mark]*.

(ii) Flood plain zoning prevents people building on parts of a flood plain that are likely to flood *[1 mark]*. It reduces the risk of flooding because impermeable surfaces aren't created, e.g. buildings and roads *[1 mark]*. It also reduces the impact of flooding because there aren't any houses or roads to be damaged *[1 mark]*.

(c) They cost less money to build and maintain *[1 mark]* and they don't damage the environment as much *[1 mark]*.

(d) E.g. there's less money to spend on flood protection and to help people after a flood in LEDCs *[1 mark]*. / More people live and work in areas that are likely to flood *[1 mark]*. / Poorer transport links mean it's more difficult to get help to places that have been affected *[1 mark]*.

(e) This question is level marked. There are also 3 extra marks available for spelling, punctuation and grammar. HINTS:
- Make sure your spelling, punctuation and grammar is consistently correct, that your meaning is clear and that you use a range of geographical terms correctly.
- Start by naming the rivers you've decided to write about and give an example of when the rivers flooded, e.g. 'The River Eden in Carlisle, England, flooded on the 8th January 2005'.
- Then describe the primary effects of the floods in each area and compare them, e.g. 'The floods killed people in both areas. Three people were killed by the Carlisle flood but a lot more people (over 2000) died as a result of the South Asia flood'.
- Next, describe and compare the secondary effects, e.g. 'One secondary effect of the floods in both areas was that children lost out on education. Although one school in Carlisle was closed for months, the impact on education was much greater in South Asia, where around 4000 schools were affected by the flood'.
- Finally, describe and compare the different flood protection measures, e.g. 'The Environment Agency monitors river levels in England and issues flood warnings to the public, local authorities and the media. Bangladesh has a Flood Forecasting and Warning System (FFWS). Flood warnings can be issued up to 72 hours before a flood occurs, however, the warnings don't reach many rural communities'.

Section Two — Coasts

Page 14 — Coastal Weathering and Erosion

1 (a) (i) Destructive waves *[1 mark]*.

(ii) They have a high frequency (10-14 waves per minute) *[1 mark]*. They are high and steep *[1 mark]*. Their backwash is more powerful than their swash *[1 mark]*.

(iii) The stronger the wind that blows over the water's surface, the larger and more powerful waves are *[1 mark]*. / The greater the distance over which the wind has blown (the fetch), the larger and more powerful waves are *[1 mark]*.

(b) Hydraulic action *[1 mark]* is when waves crash against rock and compress the air in the cracks. This puts pressure on the rock. Repeated compression widens the cracks and makes bits of rock break off *[1 mark]*. / Corrasion *[1 mark]* is when eroded particles in the water scrape and rub against rock, removing small pieces *[1 mark]*. / Attrition *[1 mark]* is when eroded particles in the water smash into each other and break into smaller fragments *[1 mark]*. / Corrosion *[1 mark]* is when seawater dissolves rock like chalk and limestone because it's a weak carbonic acid *[1 mark]*.

(c) Freeze-thaw weathering can happen when water gets into rock that has cracks *[1 mark]*. If the water freezes it expands, which puts pressure on the rock *[1 mark]*. If the water then thaws it contracts, which releases the pressure on the rock *[1 mark]*. Repeated freezing and thawing widens the cracks and causes the rock to break up *[1 mark]*.

Pages 15-17 — Coastal Landforms from Erosion

1 (a) (i) X is a wave-cut notch *[1 mark]*.
Y is unstable/overhanging rock *[1 mark]*.

Section Two — Coasts

(ii) Waves cause most erosion at the foot of a cliff *[1 mark]*. This forms a wave-cut notch (X on Figure 1), which is enlarged as erosion continues *[1 mark]*. As the notch grows, the rock above it becomes unstable (Y on Figure 1) and eventually collapses *[1 mark]*. The collapsed material is washed away and a new wave-cut notch starts to form *[1 mark]*. Repeated collapsing results in the cliff retreating *[1 mark]*. A wave-cut platform is left behind as the cliff retreats *[1 mark]*.

(iii) Geology influences the rate of cliff retreat *[1 mark]*, because soft rock or loose material is eroded very quickly, whereas hard rock is eroded much more slowly *[1 mark]*. Vegetation also influences the rate of cliff retreat *[1 mark]*, because cliffs covered in vegetation are more stable and are therefore eroded more slowly *[1 mark]*.

(b) (i) Mass movement is the shifting of rocks and loose material down a slope due to the force of gravity *[1 mark]*.

(ii) One mark for correct label and arrow on each diagram.

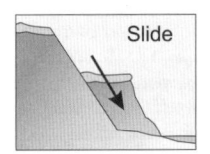

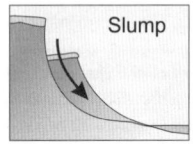

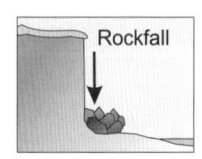

[Diagrams labelled: Slide, Slump, Rockfall]

2 (a) The landform is a cave *[1 mark]*. It was formed when waves crashing into the headland enlarged cracks in the rock — mainly by hydraulic action and corrasion *[1 mark]*. Repeated erosion and enlargement of the cracks caused a cave to form *[1 mark]*.

(b) (i) One mark for arch correctly labelled.

[Photograph with 'Arch' labelled]

(ii) An arch forms from a cave *[1 mark]*. Continued erosion deepens the cave until it breaks through the rock and forms an arch *[1 mark]*.

(c) (i) Stack *[1 mark]*.
(ii) A stack is an isolated rock that's separate from the headland *[1 mark]*.

(d) E.g. The rock supporting the arch could be eroded further, causing the arch to collapse and form a stack *[1 mark]*. The cave may be eroded further to form an arch *[1 mark]*. Also, the bay may be eroded further forming a deeper bay *[1 mark]*.

3 (a) (i) Headland *[1 mark]*.
(ii) Headlands have steep sides *[1 mark]*. / They jut out from the coastline *[1 mark]*. / They are made of resistant rock *[1 mark]*.
(iii) Headlands and bays form where there are alternating bands of resistant and less resistant rock along the coast *[1 mark]*. The less resistant rock is eroded quickly and this forms a bay *[1 mark]*. The resistant rock is eroded more slowly, forming a headland *[1 mark]*.

(b) (i) Cove *[1 mark]*.
(ii) Coves form where there is a band of hard rock along a coast with a band of softer rock behind it *[1 mark]*. Where there's a weakness in the band of hard rock, a narrow gap will be eroded *[1 mark]*. The softer rock behind will then be eroded much more to form a cove *[1 mark]*.

4 This question is level marked. There are also 3 extra marks available for spelling, punctuation and grammar. HINTS:
- Make sure your spelling, punctuation and grammar is consistently correct, that your meaning is clear and that you use a range of geographical terms correctly.
- Start by giving the details of the area you have studied, e.g. 'The Dorset coast in the south of England is made from alternating bands of hard rock (e.g. limestone and chalk) and soft rock (e.g. clay). These rocks have been eroded at different rates, leading to a range of coastal landforms'.
- Describe the erosional landforms found along the coast, and explain how each one was formed.
- You need to talk about three or four named examples, e.g. 'Lulworth Cove formed after a gap was eroded in a band of limestone, the softer clay behind was then eroded much more, forming the cove'.
- Make sure that you only talk about erosional landforms, not depositional ones.

Page 18 — Coastal Transportation and Deposition

1 (a) (i) E.g. at 0 m, the beach was wider in 2000 than it was in 2005 *[1 mark]*. At 1000 m, the beach was narrower in 2000 than 2005 *[1 mark]*. The width of the beach varied less in 2000 than it did in 2005 *[1 mark]*.

(ii) Waves follow the direction of the prevailing wind, which means they usually hit the coast at an oblique angle *[1 mark]*. The swash carries material up the beach, in the same direction as the waves *[1 mark]*. The backwash then carries material down the beach at right angles, back towards the sea *[1 mark]*. Over time, material zigzags along the coast *[1 mark]*.

(b) Traction *[1 mark]* is when large particles like boulders are pushed along the sea bed by the force of the water *[1 mark]*. / Suspension *[1 mark]* is when small particles like silt and clay are carried along in the water *[1 mark]*. / Saltation *[1 mark]* is when pebble-sized particles are bounced along the sea bed by the force of the water *[1 mark]*. / Solution *[1 mark]* is when soluble materials dissolve in the water and are carried along *[1 mark]*.

(c) (i) Deposition *[1 mark]*.
(ii) The amount of erosion elsewhere on the coast, which affects the amount of material available *[1 mark]*. The amount of transportation of material into the area *[1 mark]*.

Page 19 — Coastal Landforms from Deposition

1 (a) (i) 319898 *[1 mark]*.
(ii) 0.7 km (accept between 0.6 km and 0.8 km) *[1 mark]*.

(b) (i) Longshore drift *[1 mark]* transports sand and shingle past a sharp bend in the coastline and deposits it in the sea *[1 mark]*.
(ii) Spits and bars are both beaches formed by longshore drift *[1 mark]*. Spits stick out into the sea and are joined to the coast by one end only *[1 mark]*. Bars are connected to the coast at both ends *[1 mark]*.
(iii) A bar is connected to the coast at both ends, whereas a tombolo is connected to the coast at one end and an island at the other *[1 mark]*.

(c) It is flat, wide and has a long, gentle slope *[1 mark]*.

Section Three — Population

Page 20 — Reasons for Protecting Coastlines

1 (a) Two marks for social impacts — houses are at risk of collapsing into the sea *[1 mark]*. / Properties are damaged *[1 mark]*. / People are forced to move *[1 mark]*. / Salt from floodwater can pollute the water supply *[1 mark]*.
Two marks for economic impacts — repairing the damage caused by flooding is very expensive *[1 mark]*. / Businesses are forced to close or relocate *[1 mark]*. / Salt from the floodwater leaves farmland unusable, so farmers may lose their income *[1 mark]*.

(b) (i) 10 metres (accept between 9 and 11 metres) *[1 mark]*.
(ii) 10% (accept between 9 and 11%) *[1 mark]*.
(iii) Coastal erosion causes a loss of plant habitats *[1 mark]*. / Flooding by seawater increases the salt content of the soil, which kills plant species *[1 mark]*. / The force of floodwater uproots trees and plants *[1 mark]*. / Standing floodwater drowns some trees and plants *[1 mark]*.

Page 21 — Coastal Management Strategies

1 (a) (i) Schemes set up using knowledge of the sea and its processes to reduce the effects of flooding and erosion *[1 mark]*.
(ii) Beach replenishment *[1 mark]* creates wider beaches which slow the waves, giving greater protection from flooding and erosion *[1 mark]*. However, taking material from the seabed can kill organisms like sponges and corals *[1 mark]*. / It is an expensive defence *[1 mark]*. / It has to be repeated *[1 mark]*.

(b) (i) Building sea walls *[1 mark]* involves creating walls from hard material like concrete *[1 mark]*. / Rip rap *[1 mark]* involves piling boulders up along the coast *[1 mark]*. / Building gabions *[1 mark]* involves installing rock-filled cages at the foot of cliffs *[1 mark]*. / Buildings breakwaters *[1 mark]* involves depositing blocks or boulders on the sea bed off the coast *[1 mark]*.
(ii) Sea wall — it reflects waves back to sea, which prevents erosion of the coast *[1 mark]* and it acts as a barrier to flooding *[1 mark]*. / Rip rap/gabions — the boulders absorb wave energy and so reduce erosion and flooding *[1 mark]*. It's a fairly cheap method *[1 mark]*. / Breakwaters — force waves to break offshore *[1 mark]* so they have less erosive power when they reach the shore *[1 mark]*.
(iii) They usually cost more money to build and maintain *[1 mark]* and tend to cause more damage to the environment *[1 mark]*.

2 This question is level marked. There are also 3 extra marks available for spelling, punctuation and grammar. HINTS:
- Make sure your spelling, punctuation and grammar is <u>consistently correct</u>, that your meaning is <u>clear</u> and that you use a range of geographical terms <u>correctly</u>.
- Start by giving the <u>details</u> of the area you have studied, e.g. 'The Holderness coastline is 61 km long and stretches from Flamborough Head to Spurn Head. Erosion along the coastline is causing the cliffs to retreat'.
- Then describe the strategies that are being used and <u>explain</u> their costs and benefits.
- Give your answer a <u>logical structure</u> — fully describe each management strategy and explain its benefits and costs before moving onto the next one.
- Include <u>specific areas</u>, <u>facts</u> and <u>figures</u> in your answer, e.g. 'Defences, including two rock groynes, were built at Mappleton in 1991. They cost £2 million and protect the village and a coastal road from erosion and flooding. However, the groynes are reducing the width of beaches further down the Holderness coast, which increases erosion down the coast, e.g. Cowden Farm south of Mappleton is at risk of falling into the sea'.

Section Three — Population

Page 22 — Population Growth

1 (a) (i) 1.5 billion *[1 mark]*.
(ii) 80 years (accept anything from 75 to 85 years) *[1 mark]*.
(b) The number of live babies born per thousand of the population per year *[1 mark]*.

2 (a) One mark for all three stages labelled correctly.

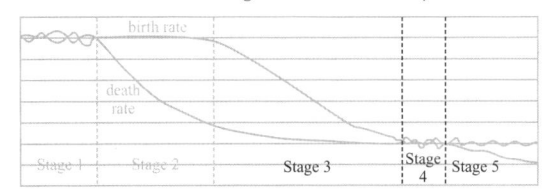

(b) (i) Birth rate in Stage 1 is high and fluctuating but in Stage 2 it is high and steady *[1 mark]*. Death rate in Stage 1 is high and fluctuating but it is falling rapidly in Stage 2 *[1 mark]*.
(ii) Population size in Stage 1 is low and steady but it is rapidly increasing in Stage 2 *[1 mark]*.
(iii) Population growth rate changes from being high in Stage 3 to zero in Stage 4 *[1 mark]*. Population growth rate is negative in Stage 5 *[1 mark]*.

Pages 23-24 — Population Growth and Structure

1 (a) The population structure of a country — how many people there are of each age group in a country *[1 mark]* and how many there are of each sex *[1 mark]*.
(b) E.g. some people are living to between 80 and 89 years *[1 mark]*. / There are more females than males and more females are living to an older age *[1 mark]*. / There is a big dip in the number of males aged 50-59 *[1 mark]*. / There are about the same number of people aged 0-9, 10-19 and 20-29 *[1 mark]*.
(c) (i) The bottom of the pyramid would become undercut with a shorter bar for the 0-9 age group *[1 mark]*. This is because fewer people are being born than in the previous generation *[1 mark]*.
(ii) The pyramid would become taller *[1 mark]* because it would include a higher age bracket, as people live to an older age *[1 mark]*. All the pyramid bars would be slightly longer *[1 mark]* as more people survive to an older age *[1 mark]*.
(d) Population growth rate is high in LEDCs *[1 mark]* because birth rates are high but death rates are falling *[1 mark]*. Population growth rate is low or negative in MEDCs *[1 mark]* because both birth rates and death rates are similarly low *[1 mark]*.

Section Three — Population

2 (a) One mark for bars drawn correctly.

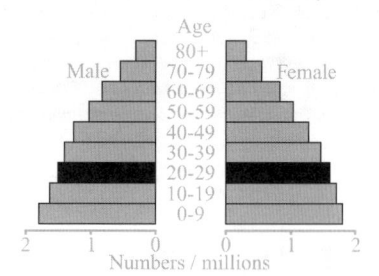

[Population pyramid showing Male/Female bars for age groups 0-9 through 80+, Numbers/millions axis from 2 to 0 to 2]

(b) E.g. countries A and B both have approximately 3.6 million people (1.8 million males and 1.8 million females) aged between 0 and 9 *[1 mark]*. However, Country A has more people in every other age group *[1 mark]*. Country A has approximately 0.6 million people (0.3 million males and 0.3 million females) aged over 80 *[1 mark]*, whereas no-one lives over the age of 79 in Country B *[1 mark]*. The population of Country A is approximately 22 million people *[1 mark]*, whereas the population of Country B is approximately 15 million people *[1 mark]*.

(c) Stage 4 *[1 mark]*, because there are a similar number of younger people and middle-aged people, which suggests a low birth rate *[1 mark]*, and there are many people surviving to quite an old age *[1 mark]*.

(d) Birth rate falls due to the emancipation of women *[1 mark]*. Better education and more widespread use of contraception means more women work instead of having children *[1 mark]*. The economy also changes from agriculture to manufacturing, so fewer children are needed to work on farms *[1 mark]*.

(e) Death rate is high at Stage 1 due to poor healthcare or famine *[1 mark]*, it then falls during Stage 2 due to improved healthcare and diet *[1 mark]*. Death rate continues to fall in Stage 3 because of medical advances *[1 mark]*.

Page 25-26 — Overpopulation

1 (a) (i) One mark for circle drawn correctly.

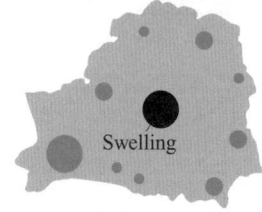

[Map showing settlements with "Swelling" labelled]

(ii) There was rapid population growth *[1 mark]* / the number of people increased from 1.4 million people to 4.4 million people *[1 mark]* / in 2000 there were two cities with at least 1 million people *[1 mark]* / there were four brand new settlements with at least 100 000 people in 2000 *[1 mark]* / four settlements grew from populations of 100 000 to 500 000 *[1 mark]*.

(iii) When there are too many people for the resources *[1 mark]*.

(b) Two marks for two social impacts, e.g. services like healthcare and education might not be able to cope with the increase so not everybody has access to them *[1 mark]* / children may miss out on education if they have to work to help support a large family *[1 mark]* / people may be forced to live in makeshift houses or overcrowded settlements *[1 mark]* / health problems may arise if not everyone has access to clean water *[1 mark]* / there may be food shortages if the country can't grow or import enough food for the population *[1 mark]*.

Two marks for two economic impacts, e.g. unemployment increases because there aren't enough jobs for the number of people in the country *[1 mark]*. Poverty increases because more people are born into families that are already poor *[1 mark]*.

(c) (i) E.g. low life expectancy and a high birth rate *[1 mark]*.

(ii) The dependency ratio becomes higher with a more youthful population *[1 mark]* because there are more people under 15 who are dependent on the working population (15-64) *[1 mark]*.

2 (a) Increased waste / too much waste for landfill sites *[1 mark]*.

(b) Developing in a way that allows people today to get the things they need *[1 mark]*, but without stopping people in the future from getting what they need *[1 mark]*.

(c) E.g. birth control programmes slow the population growth rate by reducing birth rate *[1 mark]*. Birth rate is reduced by having laws about how many children couples are allowed to have / helping couples to plan how many children to have / offering free contraception and sex education *[1 mark]*. This helps to achieve sustainable development because it means there won't be many more people using up resources today, so there will be some left for future generations *[1 mark]*.

(d) (i) By limiting the number of people who are allowed to immigrate *[1 mark]*. By limiting the number of immigrants who are of child-bearing age, so that there will be fewer immigrants having children *[1 mark]*.

(ii) It means there will be fewer people using up resources today, so there will be some left for future generations *[1 mark]*.

3 This question is level marked. There are also 3 extra marks available for spelling, punctuation and grammar. HINTS:
- *Make sure your spelling, punctuation and grammar is <u>consistently correct</u>, that your meaning is <u>clear</u> and that you use a range of geographical terms <u>correctly</u>.*
- *If you know a good <u>example</u>, pick a country that's used <u>more than one</u> strategy, then you'll have lots to write about.*
- *Start off by <u>explaining why</u> the country needs a population policy, e.g. 'China has the largest population of any country in the world — over 1.3 billion people. At times in the past, the population has been too large for China's resources, e.g. there was a disastrous famine from 1958 to 1961'.*
- *Next <u>describe</u> a bit about <u>each</u> of the strategies the country has used, e.g. 'The 'late, long, few' policy was used between 1970 and 1979. It aimed to reduce natural population growth by encouraging people to have children later, leave longer gaps between each child, and to have fewer children in total'.*
- *Explain whether the policies have been <u>successful</u> and if they're <u>sustainable</u>. E.g. 'China's one-child policy has prevented up to 400 million births. The population hasn't grown as fast so fewer resources have been used up, helping towards sustainable development'.*

Pages 27-28 — Ageing Populations

1 (a) (i) 50-59 years *[1 mark]*.

(ii) E.g. there are about 6-7 million people over the age of 60 compared to about 4-5 million people below the age of 20 *[1 mark]*.

(iii) Countries with ageing populations are usually in Stage 5 of the DTM *[1 mark]*.

(b) (i) There's a high proportion of older people who are dependent on the working population *[1 mark]*.

Section Three — Population

(ii) The birth rate of a country may drop *[1 mark]*, e.g. as people can't afford to have lots of children when they have dependent older relatives *[1 mark]*.

(c) Social impacts — e.g. healthcare services are stretched more *[1 mark]* because older people need more medical care *[1 mark]*. / People may need to spend more time working as unpaid carers for older family members *[1 mark]*. This means that members of the working population have less leisure time and are more stressed and worried *[1 mark]*. / People may have fewer children because they can't afford lots of children when they have dependent older relatives *[1 mark]*. This can lead to a drop in birth rate *[1 mark]*. /
Economic impacts — e.g. more old people means government provided pensions are smaller *[1 mark]*. People may have to retire later because they can't afford to get by on a state pension *[1 mark]*. / Taxes tend to go up *[1 mark]* because there are more pensions to pay for, and older people need more healthcare *[1 mark]*. / The economy of the country tends to grow more slowly *[1 mark]* because more money is being spent on things that don't help the economy to grow, e.g. retirement homes *[1 mark]*.

2 (a) (i) E.g. the population of Country A increased quickly between 1960 and 1980, from 50.3 million to 56.4 million *[1 mark]*. / It increased more slowly between 1980 and 2000, from 56.4 million to 57.2 million *[1 mark]*. / After 2000 the population of Country A started to decrease *[1 mark]*.

(ii) One mark for graph completed correctly.

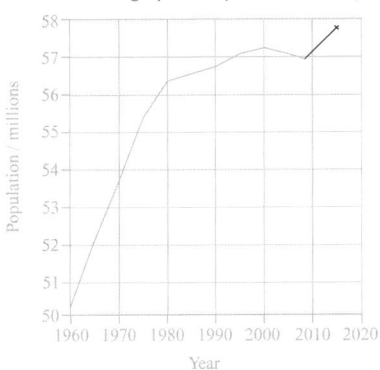

(b) (i) This strategy may increase the number of young people *[1 mark]*, which means that when they start to work there will be a larger working population to pay taxes and support the ageing population *[1 mark]*.

(ii) The strategy is not a sustainable way of managing the country's population *[1 mark]* because it increases population size so more resources are used up *[1 mark]*.

(c) Encouraging the immigration of young people from other countries *[1 mark]*. This strategy would not help towards sustainable development because it would increase the population size of the country *[1 mark]*. / Raising the retirement age *[1 mark]*. This strategy would help towards sustainable development because it would help to solve the impacts of an ageing population without increasing the population size *[1 mark]*. / Raising taxes *[1 mark]*. This strategy would help towards sustainable development because it would help to solve the impacts of an ageing population without increasing the population size *[1 mark]*.

3 This question is level marked. There are also 3 extra marks available for spelling, punctuation and grammar. HINTS:
- *Make sure your spelling, punctuation and grammar is consistently correct, that your meaning is clear and that you use a range of geographical terms correctly.*
- *Explain why the country has an ageing population, giving plenty of facts and figures. E.g. for the UK, 'People are living longer because of advances in medicine and improved living standards. Life expectancy rose between 1980 and 2006 by 2.6 years for women and 6.4 years for men. This means the proportion of older people in the population is going up'.*
- *Describe the problems that an ageing population causes, e.g. more elderly people live in poverty, the health service is put under pressure, etc.*
- *Describe some of the strategies used to cope and explain if they're working. If you can't tell whether the strategies have been successful yet, explain why.*

Page 29 — Migration

1 (a) (i) The movement of people into an area *[1 mark]*.
(ii) Between 11 and 20 thousand people *[1 mark]*.
(iii) One mark for correctly drawn arrow.

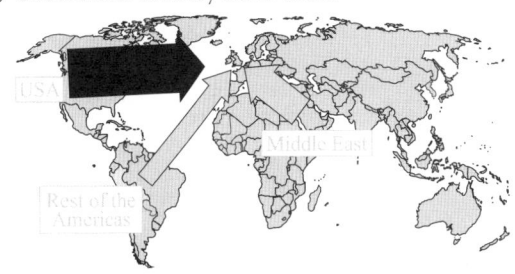

(b) (i) Push factors are the things about a person's place of origin that make them decide to move *[1 mark]*. Push factors are negative things, e.g. not being able to find a job / poor living conditions / war etc. *[1 mark]*. Pull factors are things about a person's destination that attracts them *[1 mark]*. Pull factors are positive things, e.g. higher wages / better standard of living / better healthcare etc. *[1 mark]*.

(ii) Economic factor, e.g. a shortage of jobs / low wages *[1 mark]*.
Social factor, e.g. a better standard of living / better healthcare / better education *[1 mark]*.

(c) E.g. they might emigrate to the UK as it's a safer place to live, with no wars and little risk of natural disasters *[1 mark]*.

Page 30 — Impacts of International Migration

1 (a) (i) 2003-2004 *[1 mark]*.
(ii) Between 2001 and 2002 the number of immigrants stayed steady at around 165 000 *[1 mark]*. It then fell each year between 2003 and 2005 to 137 000 in 2005 *[1 mark]*, before increasing to 146 200 in 2006 *[1 mark]*.

(b) (i) There's a bigger labour force as young people immigrate to find work *[1 mark]*. Migrant workers pay taxes that can help to fund services *[1 mark]*.

(ii) There can be less pressure on services like hospitals as there are fewer people *[1 mark]*. / Money is often sent back to the country of origin by emigrants *[1 mark]*. / There can be a shortage of labour in the country of origin as it's mostly people of working age that emigrate *[1 mark]*. / There can be a shortage of skills in the country of origin as it tends to be the most skilled and educated people who emigrate *[1 mark]*. / There may be a high proportion of older people left, who can't work and often need care *[1 mark]*.

Section Four — Settlement

(c) E.g. points-based systems let countries choose who they want to let in *[1 mark]*. People who want to move are given points for things like age, education, work experience and whether they speak the language *[1 mark]*. Only those with enough points are allowed in *[1 mark]*, so in theory only the most skilled immigrants who'll adapt well are allowed to enter *[1 mark]*.

2 This question is level marked. There are also 3 extra marks available for spelling, punctuation and grammar. HINTS:
- Make sure your spelling, punctuation and grammar is <u>consistently correct</u>, that your meaning is <u>clear</u> and that you use a range of geographical terms <u>correctly</u>.
- Start your answer by <u>introducing</u> the <u>two countries</u> you've chosen to write about and say a bit about <u>why</u> people are migrating.
- Then describe the <u>economic</u>, <u>social</u> and <u>political impacts</u> of the migration on the <u>source</u> and the <u>destination countries</u>. E.g. 'Most of the people who left Poland were young. This led to an ageing population in Poland. But the young people who left didn't need houses or jobs any more, which helped with the housing shortages and unemployment problems in Poland. One social impact in the UK was that some people were unhappy about the large numbers of Polish immigrants'.
- Finally, describe what is being done to <u>manage</u> the international migration. Write about any <u>schemes</u> that are in place to reduce the number of immigrants, or any <u>border controls</u>. E.g. 'After allowing unlimited migration from Poland, the UK Government has tightened the control of migration from some of the newer EU states, e.g. immigrants from Romania have to get permission from the Home Office to work in the UK'.

Section Four — Settlement
Page 31 — Urbanisation

1 (a) (i) Graph completed correctly *[1 mark]*.

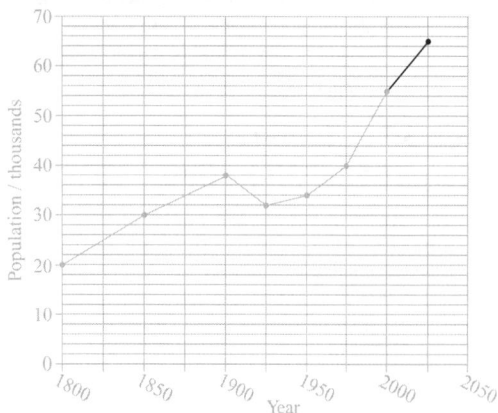

(ii) The population steadily increased from 20 000 in 1800 to 38 000 in 1900 *[1 mark]*. The population then decreased to 32 000 in 1925 *[1 mark]*, and then increased again to about 55 000 in 2000 *[1 mark]*.

(b) (i) The movement of people from the countryside to cities *[1 mark]*.

(ii) E.g. the mechanisation of farming is leading to the loss of jobs in rural areas, so people leave to look for work *[1 mark]*. / The jobs in rural areas are often low paid, which can lead to poverty, so people leave to look for better paid work *[1 mark]*. / There's often no access to services or very poor services in rural areas *[1 mark]*. / Poor harvests and crop failures can mean that people in LEDCs who are subsistence farmers make no income and may risk starvation, so they leave the countryside to look for other work *[1 mark]*.

(iii) E.g. there are more jobs available in cities than in the countryside *[1 mark]*. / The jobs in cities pay more than jobs in the countryside *[1 mark]*. / The jobs in cities offer a more stable income than jobs in the countryside *[1 mark]*. / There is better access to services like healthcare in cities *[1 mark]*.

(iv) Many young people move to urban areas for work. They then have children, which increases the proportion of the population living in urban areas *[1 mark]*. Better healthcare in urban areas means people live longer, also increasing the proportion of people living in urban areas *[1 mark]*.

Page 32-33 — Impacts of Urbanisation

1 (a) (i) A badly built, illegal settlement found in or around a city *[1 mark]*.

(ii) E.g. there are no basic services like electricity or sewers *[1 mark]*. / There are no paved roads *[1 mark]*. / The houses are overcrowded, with little space in between each house *[1 mark]*. / The houses are built from waste materials, like plastic sheets *[1 mark]*.

(b) E.g. shortage of jobs *[1 mark]*. / Shortage of housing *[1 mark]*. / Increased traffic *[1 mark]*. / Increased pollution *[1 mark]*. / Increased waste *[1 mark]*.

2 (a) 28 years *[1 mark]*.

(b) It may have been mainly young people who moved from the countryside to the cities, leaving Bhurton with an older population *[1 mark]*.

(c) E.g. urbanisation would have reduced the population of Bhurton, which might have caused shops and services in Bhurton to close due to less demand *[1 mark]*.

3 (a) (i) 1500 *[1 mark]*.

(ii) 14 *[1 mark]*.

(iii) The use of cars dropped dramatically *[1 mark]*. / More people cycled and used public transport *[1 mark]*. / Public transport options increased to include trams and hydrogen buses *[1 mark]*.

(b) They're trying to tackle housing shortages by building 500 more new houses in 2005 than in 1995 *[1 mark]*. They're trying to tackle an increase in waste by building 14 more recycling sites *[1 mark]*. They're trying to tackle traffic congestion by improving public transport *[1 mark]*. They're trying to reduce pollution by encouraging people to use more environmentally-friendly transport like trams, hydrogen buses and bicycles *[1 mark]*.

(c) E.g. they could invest in local services, which would provide jobs for local people *[1 mark]*. / They could give loans or grants to businesses if they move to rural areas, which would create jobs for local people *[1 mark]*. / They could improve public transport links so that people could get a job in the city but would still be able to live in the countryside *[1 mark]*.

Section Four — Settlement

4   This question is level marked. There are also 3 extra marks available for spelling, punctuation and grammar. HINTS:
- Make sure your spelling, punctuation and grammar is <u>consistently correct</u>, that your meaning is <u>clear</u> and that you use a range of geographical terms <u>correctly</u>.
- Start off by describing the <u>causes</u> of urbanisation in your chosen location — remember to include the <u>rural push factors</u> as well as the <u>urban pull factors</u>. E.g. 'In China there is a shortage of services pushing people out of the rural areas, and higher waged jobs attracting them to urban areas'.
- Describe the <u>impacts</u> of urbanisation in the <u>urban</u> areas. Then describe the impacts of urbanisation in the <u>rural</u> areas.
- Include both <u>positive</u> and <u>negative</u> impacts. E.g. 'Urbanisation in China has increased trade and industry in urban areas, but has also increased pollution'.
- Finish your answer by explaining how the impacts of urbanisation are being <u>managed</u>. Again, start with how urban impacts are being managed and then move on to how rural impacts are being managed — this will help you to structure your answer in a logical order, making it easier for the examiner to read.

Page 34 — Counter-urbanisation

1 (a)   The movement of people out of cities and into rural areas *[1 mark]*.
  (b)   There are good transport links so people can live in Little Yeoton and easily commute to work in the city *[1 mark]*. / Little Yeoton is an attractive place to live, with lower pollution and crime than in the city *[1 mark]*.
  (c)   E.g. houses in rural areas can cost less than in cities *[1 mark]*. / The growth of IT means more people can work at home, so don't need to live in the city *[1 mark]*. / New out-of-town business parks mean more jobs are available outside cities *[1 mark]*.
  (d)   E.g. the increased demand for houses may drive prices up. If young people can't afford to buy a house they'll have to move away, which can lead to resentment *[1 mark]*. Commuters may prefer to use shops and services closer to work, so local ones could shut down due to lack of demand, which isolates local people without transport *[1 mark]*. Commuter villages are empty during the day, which can cause a decline in community spirit *[1 mark]*.
  (e)   E.g. the local government could make policies to provide more houses for local people, which would stop commuters buying houses *[1 mark]*. / They could invest in services in commuter villages, so they don't close down *[1 mark]*. / They could regenerate areas in Hamslow to make them more attractive, so fewer people would leave and some may return to the city *[1 mark]*.

Pages 35-36 — Urban Land Use

1 (a) (i)   Photo A: CBD / central business district *[1 mark]*.
Photo B: Suburbs *[1 mark]*.
Photo C: Rural-urban fringe *[1 mark]*.
Photo D: Inner city *[1 mark]*.
  (b) (i)   Low-class housing *[1 mark]* and industry *[1 mark]*.
      (ii)   There's low-class housing as small houses were built near factories for workers *[1 mark]*.
  (c) (i)   E.g. high-class housing *[1 mark]*.
      (ii)   There is high-class housing because richer people who like a rural lifestyle and being in reach of the city want to live there *[1 mark]*. Land is cheaper, meaning that bigger houses can be built *[1 mark]*.

2 (a)   One mark for each correct label.

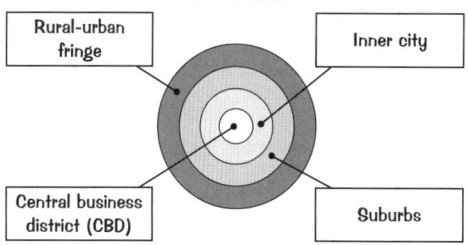

(Diagram labels: Rural-urban fringe; Inner city; Central business district (CBD); Suburbs)

  (b) (i)   E.g. shops *[1 mark]* and offices *[1 mark]*.
      (ii)   The CBD is busy and very accessible *[1 mark]*. Land is expensive, so only businesses can afford it *[1 mark]*.
  (c)   The suburbs are less crowded and more pleasant, with less traffic and pollution *[1 mark]*.
  (d)   E.g. shopping centres are built out of town *[1 mark]*. Inner city tower blocks are removed and replaced with housing estates on the rural-urban fringe *[1 mark]*.

Page 37 — Urban Development

1 (a) (i)   100% - 82% = 18% *[1 mark]*.
      (ii)   It decreased from 150 hectares to 100 hectares *[1 mark]*.
      (iii)   One mark for table correctly completed.

Year	Housing available	No. of people on housing list	Housing deficit
1992	9000	12 000	3000
2000	7500	23 000	15 500
2008	14 000	18 000	4000

  (b) (i)   More housing is needed *[1 mark]*. More jobs are needed *[1 mark]*. More green spaces are needed *[1 mark]*.
      (ii)   E.g. new housing could be built on brownfield sites *[1 mark]*, so that green spaces are not used up *[1 mark]*. New houses could be made carbon-neutral *[1 mark]* to reduce pollution and conserve resources *[1 mark]*.

2   This question is level marked. There are also 3 extra marks available for spelling, punctuation and grammar. HINTS:
- Make sure your spelling, punctuation and grammar is <u>consistently correct</u>, that your meaning is <u>clear</u> and that you use a range of geographical terms <u>correctly</u>.
- Start off by giving a bit of <u>background</u> on the <u>area</u> you've chosen. Explain <u>where</u> it is and <u>why</u> it needs to be developed.
- <u>Describe</u> the <u>development</u> of the area in plenty of detail. E.g. 'The Gorbals in Glasgow are being regenerated and £170 million is being invested. There's an ongoing project to build a new 'urban village' with over 1500 new homes, a shopping centre, a library, a community centre and a good quality bus service.'
- Then explain whether the development is <u>sustainable</u>. E.g. 'The development is on derelict, brownfield sites, which saves land for future generations to use, making it more sustainable than building on greenfield sites.'

Page 38 — Retail Services

1 (a) (i)   Low order goods *[1 mark]*.
      (ii)   High order goods are bought occasionally and are usually more expensive, e.g. furniture and cars *[1 mark]*. Low order goods are bought frequently and are usually cheap, e.g. milk and newspapers *[1 mark]*.

Section Five — Tectonic Hazards

(b) The shops in Figure 1 are likely to have a high threshold population because they sell high order goods and the rent is expensive *[1 mark]*. The shop in Figure 2 is likely to have a low threshold population because it sells low order goods and the rent is cheap *[1 mark]*.
(c) (i) The area that people come from to visit a shop or an area *[1 mark]*.
   (ii) They sell expensive goods that are only bought occasionally, so people are prepared to travel from a wide area *[1 mark]*.
(d) E.g. often located in the suburbs *[1 mark]*. / Sell a mixture of high and low order goods *[1 mark]*. / Medium threshold population *[1 mark]*. / Medium sphere of influence *[1 mark]*.

Page 39 — Changing Retail Services

1 (a) (i) 5 miles *[1 mark]*.
   (ii) 4 miles *[1 mark]*.
(b) (i) The distance people travelled to do their weekly shopping increased from an average of 1.5 miles in 1960 to an average of 9.5 miles in 2000 *[1 mark]*. There has been a bigger increase in recent years, from 1985 to 2000 *[1 mark]*.
   (ii) E.g. car ownership has increased, so people can travel further for their shopping *[1 mark]*.
   (iii) There may be fewer smaller convenience stores in rural areas *[1 mark]*. There may be more out-of-town shopping centres *[1 mark]*.
(c) People now want a larger range of goods at cheaper prices *[1 mark]*. Smaller, specialist shops can't meet this demand *[1 mark]*, but larger chain stores and supermarkets can *[1 mark]*. So there may be fewer smaller, specialist shops and more chain stores and supermarkets *[1 mark]*.
2 This question is level marked. There are also 3 extra marks available for spelling, punctuation and grammar. HINTS:
- *Make sure your spelling, punctuation and grammar is <u>consistently correct</u>, that your meaning is <u>clear</u> and that you use a range of geographical terms <u>correctly</u>.*
- *<u>Describe how</u> the nature of retail services has <u>changed</u> over time in your chosen area and include plenty of <u>details</u>. E.g. 'A large out-of-town shopping centre called Meadowhall was built near Sheffield in 1990. The centre has 280 shops, is easily accessible by car and has 12 000 free parking spaces. Some shops in Sheffield city centre have closed down, possibly because shoppers are going to Meadowhall instead'.*
- *Include <u>ongoing changes</u> to the area's retail services, e.g. 'Sheffield city centre is being redeveloped by providing more parking and setting up a 'City Watch' scheme to reduce crime. Planners hope to encourage shoppers back to the city centre'.*

Section Five — Tectonic Hazards

Page 40 — Tectonic Hazards and Tectonic Plates

1 (a) (i) A naturally occurring event that has the potential to affect people's lives or property *[1 mark]*.
   (ii) E.g. earthquake *[1 mark]*.

(b) (i) One mark for each correct label.

(Labels: Crust, Outer core, Inner core, Mantle)

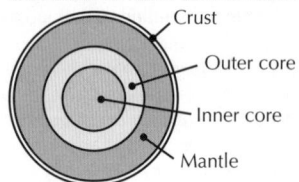

   (ii) Continental crust is thicker than oceanic crust *[1 mark]*. Continental crust is less dense than oceanic crust *[1 mark]*.
   (iii) Because the mantle beneath them is moving *[1 mark]*.
   (iv) Plate margins/plate boundaries *[1 mark]*.

Page 41 — Types of Tectonic Plate Margins

1 (a) (i) Plate margin A is a constructive plate margin *[1 mark]*. As the two plates move away from each other, magma rises from the mantle to fill the gap *[1 mark]*. The magma then cools, creating new crust *[1 mark]*.
   (ii) A conservative plate margin *[1 mark]*.
   (iii) Plates could move sideways past each other *[1 mark]* or move in the same direction but at different speeds *[1 mark]*.
(b) (i) A destructive plate margin *[1 mark]*.
   (ii) One mark for each correct label.

(Labels: ocean trench, volcano, oceanic plate, continental plate)

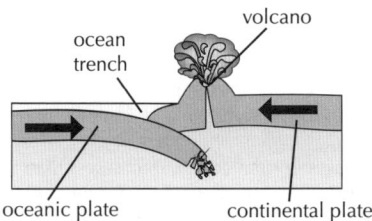

Pages 42-43 — The Distribution of Tectonic Hazards

1 (a) Almost all earthquakes are found along plate margins *[1 mark]* but some (very few) occur in the middle of plates *[1 mark]*.
(b) Tension builds up *[1 mark]* as one plate gets stuck as it's moving down past the other into the mantle *[1 mark]*. The plates eventually jerk past each other *[1 mark]*, sending out shockwaves *[1 mark]*.
2 (a) (i) The focus is the point in the Earth where the earthquake starts *[1 mark]*.
   (ii) 17 km *[1 mark]*
(b) One mark for epicentre correctly labelled on the surface directly above the focus.

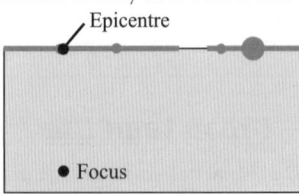

(Diagram with Epicentre labelled on surface above Focus)

(c) The Richter scale *[1 mark]*.
3 (a) Volcanoes are concentrated along destructive plate margins *[1 mark]* and constructive plate margins *[1 mark]*. Some also occur away from any plate margins (e.g. in Hawaii) *[1 mark]* and on conservative plate margins *[1 mark]*.
(b) A destructive plate margin *[1 mark]*. The oceanic plate moves down into the mantle, where it's melted and destroyed *[1 mark]*. A pool of magma forms, and the magma rises through cracks in the crust called vents *[1 mark]*. The magma erupts onto the surface, forming a volcano *[1 mark]*.

Section Five — Tectonic Hazards

(c) The North Atlantic ridge is located on a constructive plate margin *[1 mark]*. The magma rises up into the gap created by the plates moving apart, forming a volcano *[1 mark]*.

(d) Some volcanoes form over parts of the mantle that are really hot *[1 mark]*, called hotspots *[1 mark]*.

Page 44 — Impacts of Earthquakes

1 (a) Many people were killed or injured *[1 mark]*. / Buildings were destroyed *[1 mark]*. / Roads were damaged *[1 mark]*.

(b) E.g. the earthquake triggered landslides *[1 mark]*. Landslides blocked the roads, meaning that rescue teams could not reach some areas *[1 mark]*. / People were left homeless *[1 mark]*. / People were left without clean water *[1 mark]*. / People were left without medical aid *[1 mark]*.

(c) People are employed in the area. If they moved away they would have to find new jobs *[1 mark]*. / People have always lived in the area, so moving away would mean leaving family and friends *[1 mark]*. / People are confident of support from their government after an earthquake, e.g. to help rebuild houses *[1 mark]*. / Some people think that severe earthquakes won't happen again in the area, so it's safe to live there *[1 mark]*.

(d) E.g. there is more poor quality housing in LEDCs *[1 mark]*. Poor quality houses are less stable, so they're more easily destroyed by earthquakes *[1 mark]*. / The infrastructure is often poorer in LEDCs *[1 mark]*. Poor quality roads make it harder for emergency services to reach injured people, which leads to more deaths *[1 mark]*. / LEDCs don't have much money to protect against earthquakes, e.g. by making buildings earthquake proof *[1 mark]*, so more buildings are destroyed *[1 mark]*. / LEDCs don't have enough money or resources (e.g. food and emergency vehicles) to react straight away to earthquakes *[1 mark]*, so more people are affected by the secondary impacts *[1 mark]*. / Healthcare is often worse in LEDCs *[1 mark]*. Many hospitals in LEDCs don't have enough supplies to deal with the large numbers of casualties after an earthquake, so more people die from treatable injuries *[1 mark]*.

2 This question is level marked. There are also 3 extra marks available for spelling, punctuation and grammar. HINTS:
- Make sure your spelling, punctuation and grammar is <u>consistently correct</u>, that your meaning is <u>clear</u> and that you use a range of geographical terms <u>correctly</u>.
- <u>State</u> the tectonic hazard (e.g. earthquake) and give details of <u>two specific events</u> — one in a <u>MEDC</u> and one in a <u>LEDC</u>. State <u>where</u> and <u>when</u> they occurred and their <u>magnitude</u> on the Richter scale. E.g. 'An earthquake measuring 6.3 on the Richter scale hit L'Aquila in Italy on the 6th April 2009'.
- <u>Compare</u> the impact of the hazard on the two countries, focusing on the <u>differences</u> between the two. Use <u>plenty of facts</u> — e.g. how many people were affected, the cost of the damage, the primary and secondary impacts of each event. For each impact, <u>discuss one location first, then the other</u>, e.g. 'The death toll in L'Aquila was around 290, whereas in Kashmir it was around 80 000'.
- <u>Explain why</u> the impacts were so different in the two countries — mention <u>differences</u> in things like planning laws, infrastructure, medical care, emergency aid and education. Again, discuss one location first, then the other, e.g. 'In Italy, camps were rapidly set up for injured people, providing food, shelter and medical care. In contrast, poorly constructed roads in Kashmir slowed down rescue and aid efforts, meaning that help didn't arrive for days or weeks. This increased the death toll'.

Page 45 — Reducing the Impacts of Earthquakes

1 (a) (i) Location C is most suitable *[1 mark]*, because it is furthest away from the plate margin *[1 mark]* and has not experienced any earthquakes in the past *[1 mark]*.

(ii) E.g. buildings can be designed to withstand earthquakes, e.g. by using materials like reinforced concrete *[1 mark]*. Firebreaks can be made to reduce the spread of fires caused by earthquakes *[1 mark]*.

(b) E.g. the government could educate people about what to do if there is an earthquake, e.g. how to evacuate *[1 mark]*. / Emergency services could train and prepare for earthquakes, e.g. by practising rescuing people from collapsed buildings and stockpiling medicine *[1 mark]*. / People can be told how to make a survival kit containing essential items *[1 mark]*. / Governments can plan evacuation routes to get people out of dangerous areas quickly and safely after an earthquake *[1 mark]*.

(c) (i) Sustainable strategies meet the needs of people today without stopping people in the future meeting their needs *[1 mark]*, so they must be effective, not damage the environment and not cost too much *[1 mark]*.

(ii) Predicting earthquakes is not a sustainable strategy *[1 mark]*, because it is currently impossible to predict when an earthquake will occur, so it isn't effective *[1 mark]*.

(iii) E.g. mapping previous earthquakes shows areas likely to be affected in future *[1 mark]*. / Lots of small tremors in the area *[1 mark]*. / Cracks appearing in rocks *[1 mark]*. / Strange animal behaviour, e.g. rats abandoning nests *[1 mark]*.

Page 46 — Impacts of Volcanoes

1 (a) (i) Vesuvius attracts lots of tourists, providing jobs in the tourist industry *[1 mark]*. The soil around Vesuvius is fertile so it's good for farming, which attracts farmers *[1 mark]*.

(ii) E.g. volcanoes are a source of geothermal energy, which can be used to generate electricity, so people live near them to work at power stations *[1 mark]*.

(iii) The more settlements built and businesses set up in an area, the greater the impact because there are more people and properties to be affected by the eruption *[1 mark]*.

(b) E.g. people and animals may be killed or injured by pyroclastic flows, lava flows and falling rocks *[1 mark]*. / Roads and buildings may be damaged by pyroclastic flows, lava flows and falling ash *[1 mark]*. / Crops may be damaged by falling ash *[1 mark]*. / Water supplies may be contaminated by falling ash *[1 mark]*. / People, animals and plants may be suffocated by carbon dioxide *[1 mark]*.

(c) E.g. mudflows form when volcanic material mixes with water from, e.g. rainfall or snow melt *[1 mark]*. Mudflows can kill or injure people or bury houses and land *[1 mark]*. / Fires are started by lava flows and pyroclastic flows *[1 mark]*, which then spread and cause more damage *[1 mark]*. / Crop damage *[1 mark]* causes a shortage of food *[1 mark]*. / People are left homeless *[1 mark]* when houses are destroyed *[1 mark]*. / People are left unemployed *[1 mark]* when businesses are destroyed *[1 mark]*. / Roads are blocked or destroyed *[1 mark]*, so aid and emergency vehicles can't get through *[1 mark]*. / Sulfur dioxide released into the atmosphere *[1 mark]* causes acid rain *[1 mark]*.

Section Six — Climatic Hazards

(d) E.g. poor quality roads make it harder for emergency services to reach injured people, which leads to more deaths *[1 mark]*. / LEDCs don't have enough money or resources (e.g. food and emergency vehicles) to react straight away to volcanic eruptions *[1 mark]*. / Many hospitals in LEDCs don't have enough supplies to deal with the large numbers of casualties after an eruption, so more people die from treatable injuries *[1 mark]*.

Pages 47-48 — Reducing the Impacts of Volcanoes

1 (a) (i) Magma had built up under the crater floor *[1 mark]*.
(ii) The tilt of the crater floor decreased from 0.16° to 0.11° *[1 mark]*. This could have been caused by the bulge getting smaller as magma erupted *[1 mark]*.
(b) (i) 230 tonnes *[1 mark]*.
(ii) One mark for line drawn correctly.

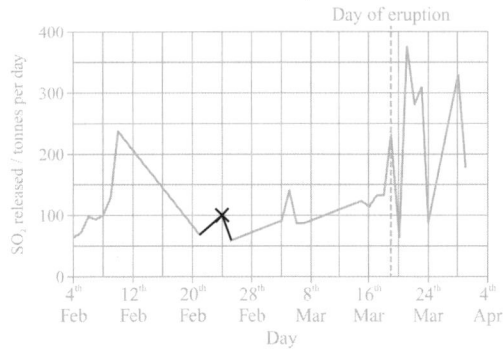

(c) The change in the tilt of the crater floor gave a better warning of when the volcano was going to erupt *[1 mark]*. This is because it increased very quickly just before the eruption, whereas sulfur dioxide emissions didn't increase quickly in the days before the eruption *[1 mark]*.
(d) E.g. they could monitor tiny earthquakes that happen before eruptions *[1 mark]*.
(e) Prediction is a sustainable strategy *[1 mark]*, because although it is expensive, it can be effective and is environmentally friendly *[1 mark]*.
2 (a) (i) If the earth barriers divert lava flow away from developed areas *[1 mark]*, it would decrease the number of people killed or injured and reduce damage to houses and businesses *[1 mark]*.
(ii) It is a sustainable strategy because it was effective in diverting lava flow away from developed areas *[1 mark]* and it saved more money than it cost without damaging the environment *[1 mark]*.
(iii) E.g. future developments could be planned to avoid the areas most at risk from lava flows *[1 mark]*. / Firebreaks could be made to reduce the spread of fires *[1 mark]*. / Emergency services could train and prepare for eruptions, e.g. by setting up emergency camps for homeless people *[1 mark]*. / Governments could plan evacuation routes to get people away from the volcano quickly and safely *[1 mark]*.
(b) (i) The poster tells people what items to put in a survival kit. These items help reduce the chance of people dying if they are stuck in the area after an eruption *[1 mark]*.
(ii) People can be educated about how to evacuate an area quickly and safely if a volcano erupts *[1 mark]*.

Section Six — Climatic Hazards
Page 49 — Tropical Storms

1 (a) (i) One mark for each correct label up to a maximum of four.

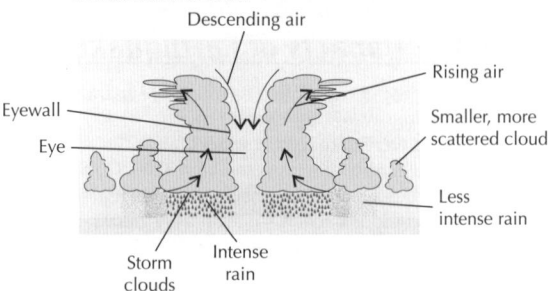

(ii) E.g. they have a circular shape *[1 mark]*. / They spin anticlockwise (in the northern hemisphere) *[1 mark]*. / They're hundreds of kilometres wide *[1 mark]*.
(b) E.g. all tropical storms form near the equator, then move westwards and away from the equator *[1 mark]*. Some tropical storms move more than 23° from the equator *[1 mark]*. They form near the equator because they only form over water that's 27 °C or higher *[1 mark]*. They move westwards because of the easterly winds near the equator *[1 mark]*. Tropical storms affect the east coast of the USA and parts of South America and central America *[1 mark]*. South Asia, east Asia and north Australia are also affected by tropical storms *[1 mark]*.
(c) Tropical storms lose strength when they move over land because the energy supply from the warm water is cut off *[1 mark]*.

Page 50 — Impacts of Tropical Storms

1 (a) (i) The number of deaths was much higher in Honduras (7000) than in the USA (1) *[1 mark]*. The number of homes destroyed was much higher in Honduras (35 000) than in the USA (173) *[1 mark]*.
(ii) One reason for the higher number of deaths in Honduras and an explanation:
E.g. the infrastructure may be poorer in Honduras *[1 mark]*. Poor quality roads make it harder for emergency services to rescue people, which leads to more deaths *[1 mark]*. / More people in Honduras may depend on farming *[1 mark]*. If crops and livestock were destroyed during the storm then people may have died of starvation *[1 mark]*. / Healthcare may be worse in Honduras *[1 mark]*. If hospitals didn't have enough supplies to deal with the large numbers of casualties then people would have died from treatable injuries *[1 mark]*.
One reason for the higher number of homes destroyed in Honduras and an explanation:
E.g. there may have been more poor quality housing in Honduras *[1 mark]*. Poor quality houses are destroyed more easily by strong winds and flooding *[1 mark]*.
(b) E.g. they've always lived there, so moving away would mean leaving friends and family *[1 mark]*. / They're employed in the area. If people move they have to find new jobs *[1 mark]*. / They're confident of support from their government after a tropical storm, e.g. to help rebuild houses *[1 mark]*. / Some people think that severe tropical storms won't happen again in the area, so it's safe to live there *[1 mark]*.

Section Six — Climatic Hazards

(c) E.g. people are left homeless *[1 mark]*. / There's a shortage of clean water and a lack of proper sanitation, so it's easier for diseases to spread *[1 mark]*. / Roads are blocked or destroyed so aid and emergency vehicles can't get through *[1 mark]*. / Businesses are damaged or destroyed, causing unemployment *[1 mark]*. / There's a shortage of food because crops are damaged and livestock has died *[1 mark]*. / People may suffer psychological problems if they knew people who died *[1 mark]*.

2 This question is level marked. There are also 3 extra marks available for spelling, punctuation and grammar. HINTS:
- Make sure your spelling, punctuation and grammar is *consistently correct*, that your meaning is *clear* and that you use a range of geographical terms *correctly*.
- Start by *describing* how the climatic hazard is caused and say a bit about its *characteristics*, e.g. 'Tropical storms develop near the equator above sea water that's 27 °C or higher. Warm, moist air rises and condensation occurs. This releases huge amounts of energy which makes the storms really powerful. They move west because of the easterly winds near the equator, but they lose strength when they move over land because the energy supply from the warm water is cut off'.
- Next say a bit about *when* and *where* your named climatic hazard occurred.
- Then talk about the *primary impacts* of the climatic hazard. These are the *immediate impacts* of the hazard, e.g. 'More than 1800 people were killed by Hurricane Katrina and 300 000 houses were destroyed. The storm left 3 million people without electricity. Coastal habitats such as sea turtle breeding beaches were damaged'.

Pages 51-52 — Reducing the Impacts of Tropical Storms

1 (a) Emergency services can train and prepare for disasters, e.g. by practising rescuing people from flooded areas with helicopters *[1 mark]*. This increases the number of people who will be rescued, so fewer people will be killed *[1 mark]*. Future developments, e.g. new houses, can be planned to avoid the areas most at risk (e.g. right on the coast) *[1 mark]*. This reduces the number of buildings destroyed by winds or flooding *[1 mark]*. Governments can plan evacuation routes to get people away from storms quickly *[1 mark]*. This reduces the number of people injured or killed *[1 mark]*.

(b) (i) To be sustainable a strategy needs to be effective, to meet the needs of people today *[1 mark]*. The strategy also can't be expensive or harm the environment too much *[1 mark]*, so it won't stop people in the future meeting their needs *[1 mark]*.

(ii) They're sustainable *[1 mark]*.

(c) Foreign governments can send aid to countries hit by tropical storms, e.g. food *[1 mark]*. This helps to reduce the impacts, e.g. food aid stops people going hungry *[1 mark]*.

2 This question is level marked. There are also 3 extra marks available for spelling, punctuation and grammar. HINTS:
- Make sure your spelling, punctuation and grammar is *consistently correct*, that your meaning is *clear* and that you use a range of geographical terms *correctly*.
- First *introduce* the climatic hazard you've named. Talk about *when* and *where* it happened.

- Then describe the *impacts* of the hazard — you can talk about the *primary* impacts, *secondary* impacts, or *both*. E.g. 'Cyclone Nargis killed more than 140 000 people. The tropical storm destroyed 450 000 houses and 1700 schools. 200 000 farm animals were killed, crops were lost and over 40% of food stores were destroyed'.
- Finally, *explain* how the country's level of *economic development* affected the *severity* of the impacts, e.g. 'Burma is an LEDC and so needed aid from foreign governments to deal with the impacts of the tropical storm. However, Burma's Government initially refused to accept any foreign aid. Aid workers were only allowed in 3 weeks after the disaster occurred. This increased the number of people killed because help for some injured people came too late'.

3 (a) (i) One mark for correct landfall location.
One mark for correctly drawn track inland.

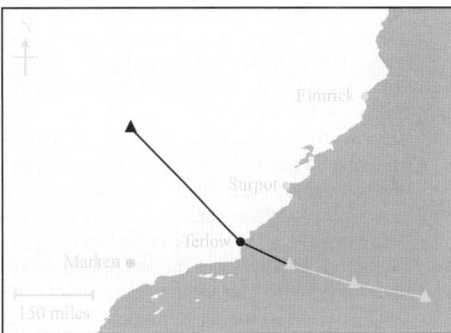

(ii) It can give people time to evacuate, which reduces the number of injuries and deaths *[1 mark]*. It can also give them time to protect their homes and businesses, e.g. by boarding up windows *[1 mark]*.

(b) (i) Gabions are more sustainable *[1 mark]*. Both methods reduce the impacts of tropical storms, but gabions are less expensive per metre *[1 mark]*.

(ii) E.g. buildings can be designed to withstand tropical storms, e.g. by using reinforced concrete *[1 mark]*. / Buildings can also be put on stilts so they're safe from floodwater *[1 mark]*. / Flood defences can be built along rivers, e.g. levees *[1 mark]*.

Page 53 — Drought

1 (a) (i) There were large areas affected by extreme drought around the equator, e.g. in central Africa *[1 mark]*. Extreme droughts also occurred around 23° S, e.g. in Australia and South America *[1 mark]* and north of 23° N, e.g. north Africa and the Middle East *[1 mark]*. There were smaller areas of extreme drought in areas of the far north, e.g. in North America and north east Asia *[1 mark]*.

(ii) Droughts are caused when changes in atmospheric circulation mean it doesn't rain much in an area, e.g. by making annual rains fail *[1 mark]*. They are also caused when high pressure weather systems called anticyclones block depressions, which cause rain *[1 mark]*.

(b) (i) 100 mm *[1 mark]*
(ii) 9 months *[1 mark]*
(iii) E.g. they've always lived there, so moving away would mean leaving friends and family *[1 mark]*. / They're employed in the area. If people move they have to find new jobs *[1 mark]*. / They're confident of support from their government after a drought *[1 mark]*. / Some people think that severe droughts won't happen again in the area, so it's safe to live there *[1 mark]*.

Section Seven — Development

Page 54 — Impacts of Droughts

1 (a) (i) Primary impacts — crops have died from a lack of water *[1 mark]*. / People have died from dehydration *[1 mark]*. / Soil has dried out so it's easily eroded by winds *[1 mark]*.
Secondary impacts — animals have died from starvation *[1 mark]*. / People may die from starvation because there's a shortage of food *[1 mark]*. / People have moved out of the area to find water *[1 mark]*. / Farms have closed, causing unemployment *[1 mark]*.
   (ii) E.g. there can be conflicts over water supplies *[1 mark]*. / People may suffer psychological problems, e.g. stress from losing their business *[1 mark]*. / Dried out vegetation can be easily ignited, e.g. by lightning, causing wildfires *[1 mark]*. / Winds pick up dry soil, causing dust storms *[1 mark]*.
(b) Overgrazing means the soil erosion caused by droughts is made worse *[1 mark]*. It reduces vegetation in an area so the soil isn't held together as strongly and can be eroded more easily *[1 mark]*. Excessive irrigation *[1 mark]* depletes rivers and lakes so there's even less water available during droughts *[1 mark]* / can cause salinisation of the soil, which means that crops don't grow very well, increasing the impact of droughts *[1 mark]*.
(c) More people in LEDCs depend on farming *[1 mark]* so if crops and livestock die lots of people will lose their livelihoods and some might starve *[1 mark]*. LEDCs have less money to prepare for droughts or respond to them, e.g. by building reservoirs *[1 mark]* so the impacts of drought are more severe *[1 mark]*.

Pages 55-56 — Reducing the Impacts of Droughts

1 (a) (i) One mark for correctly drawn line.

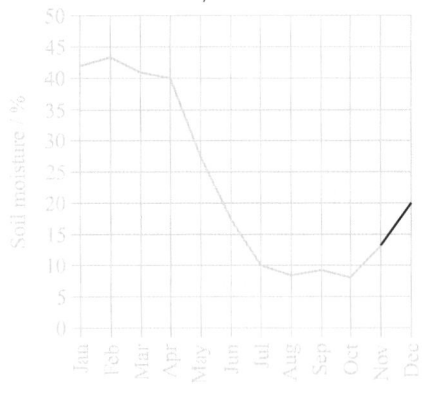

   (ii) 40 – 10 = 30% *[1 mark]*
(b) (i) E.g. monitoring rainfall / river levels *[1 mark]*.
   (ii) Prediction gives people/authorities a chance to prepare for the drought *[1 mark]*, e.g. by banning hosepipes / rationing water / moving people out of areas that will be worst affected *[1 mark]*.
(c) (i) Drip irrigation is more efficient *[1 mark]* because it uses 2.5 million litres per hectare less than furrow irrigation every year *[1 mark]*.
   (ii) It allows crops to carry on being produced but reduces the demand on water supplies *[1 mark]*.
2 (a) (i) 2001 *[1 mark]*
   (ii) They increase water supply, so more water is available during a drought *[1 mark]*. This reduces deaths from dehydration / reduces conflicts over supplies / makes food production more reliable etc. *[1 mark]*.
   (iii) E.g. building wells can be sustainable because they meet the needs of people today and are environmentally-friendly *[1 mark]*. However, wells can deplete groundwater supplies, which means there's less water for people in the future *[1 mark]*.
   (iv) Emergency aid, e.g. food / water tankers, can stop people dying from dehydration or starvation *[1 mark]*.
(b) (i) It reduces the demand on water supplies, so more water is available during a drought *[1 mark]*.
   (ii) E.g. people can reduce the amount of water they use *[1 mark]*, e.g. by installing low volume flush toilets / by having showers instead of baths *[1 mark]*. People can also collect rainwater, e.g. by installing water butts *[1 mark]*, and use it to wash their car or water their garden *[1 mark]*.

Section Seven — Development
Pages 57-58 — Measuring Development

1 (a) The total value of goods and services a country produces in a year *[1 mark]*, divided by the total population of the country *[1 mark]*.
(b) Birth rate is the number of live babies born per thousand of the population per year *[1 mark]*.
(c) GDP per capita *[1 mark]*
(d) Canada is the most developed *[1 mark]* because it has the highest GDP per capita, life expectancy rate and literacy rate *[1 mark]*. It also has the lowest infant mortality rate and relatively low birth rates and death rates *[1 mark]*.
(e) A country with a higher GDP per capita has a higher literacy rate *[1 mark]*. This is because a country that has a higher GDP per capita will have more money to spend on education *[1 mark]*.
(f) The measures can be misleading when used on their own because they are averages so they don't show up elite groups in the population or variations within the country *[1 mark]*. / Economic indicators can be inaccurate for countries where trade is informal *[1 mark]*. / Economic indicators are affected by exchange rate changes *[1 mark]*.
2 (a) The average age a person can expect to live to *[1 mark]*. It's a measure of the quality of healthcare and access to healthcare *[1 mark]*.
(b) (i) 51-55 years *[1 mark]*
   (ii) Regions with a life expectancy of less than 50 years occur in a belt from east to west across the centre of the country *[1 mark]*. This belt is interrupted in the east by a region with higher life expectancy *[1 mark]*.
(c) (i) Social *[1 mark]*
   (ii) E.g. infant mortality rate, which is the number of babies who die under one year old per thousand babies born *[1 mark]*. This is a measure of sanitation and healthcare *[1 mark]*. As a country develops, it decreases *[1 mark]*.

Page 59 — Categories of Development

1 (a) (i) More Economically Developed Country *[1 mark]*.
   (ii) MEDCs are generally found in the north, e.g. the USA, Canada and European countries *[1 mark]*. However, some MEDCs are found in the south, e.g. Australia and New Zealand *[1 mark]*. LEDCs are generally found in the south, e.g. Brazil and all the African countries *[1 mark]*.
   (iii) It doesn't show which countries are developing quickly *[1 mark]*. / It doesn't show which countries aren't really developing at all *[1 mark]*. / It is based on wealth, which doesn't always match development level *[1 mark]*.

Section Eight — Industry

(b) Newly Industrialising Countries (NICs) are rapidly getting richer as their economies move from being based on primary industry to secondary industry, e.g. China and Brazil *[1 mark]*. Most developed countries are the most developed in the world, e.g. Norway and Canada *[1 mark]*. Middle income countries are not rich but not poor. They're also developing quite quickly, e.g. Bulgaria and Poland *[1 mark]*. Least developed countries are the poorest countries with the lowest quality of life, e.g. Ethiopia and Chad *[1 mark]*.

Pages 60-62 — Factors Affecting the Level of Development

1 (a) More than twice as many people can access clean water in Pakistan than in Ethiopia *[1 mark]*.
(b) A country with limited access to clean water will be less developed *[1 mark]*. This is because if the only water people can drink is dirty they'll get ill due to waterborne diseases and this will reduce their quality of life *[1 mark]*. Ill people can't work so they don't add money to the economy and they also cost money to treat *[1 mark]*. This means the country will have less money to spend on development *[1 mark]*.
2 (a) There's a strong positive correlation *[1 mark]*.
(b) 0.39 (accept 0.38) *[1 mark]*.
(c) A low literacy rate shows the country's population is poorly educated *[1 mark]*. If a country's population is poorly educated, they can't get good jobs so will have a lower quality of life *[1 mark]*. Having a poorly paid job also means they can't add much money to the economy, so the country will have less money to spend on development *[1 mark]*.
3 (a) E.g. the building in the centre of the photo has been destroyed *[1 mark]*.
(b) Countries that have lots of natural disasters are usually less developed *[1 mark]* because natural disasters reduce quality of life for the people affected *[1 mark]*. It also costs a lot of money to rebuild after disasters occur, which reduces the amount of money the government has to spend on development projects *[1 mark]*.
4 (a) (i) 1225 million ÷ 100 x 3.0 = US$36.75 million *[1 mark]*.
(ii) 100% − 6.3% − 14.8% = 78.9% *[1 mark]*.
(iii) Nicaragua exports mostly primary products. Not much profit is made selling primary products so less money is made to spend on development *[1 mark]*. The UK exports a much higher percentage of manufacturing products than Nicaragua, which make more profit so there's more to spend on development *[1 mark]*.
(b) If a country has poor trade links it will be less developed *[1 mark]* because it won't make a lot of money so has less to spend on development *[1 mark]*.
5 (a) (i) 0.3 *[1 mark]*.
(ii) Botswana's HDI decreased from 0.68 in 1990 to 0.63 in 2000 *[1 mark]*. It then increased to about 0.67 in 2005 *[1 mark]*.
(iii) Corrupt governments allow some people in a country to get richer by breaking the law, while others stay poor *[1 mark]*. The poorer people in the country have a low quality of life because they can't afford things such as good housing, healthcare and education *[1 mark]*. Unstable governments might not invest in things like healthcare and education *[1 mark]*. Both of these things lead to slow development or no development at all *[1 mark]*.

(b) (i) Egypt's HDI was much higher than Uganda's throughout the period *[1 mark]*. However, while Egypt's HDI steadily increased in that time, Uganda's stayed constant around 0.38 from 1990 to 1995 and then increased to 0.5 in 2005 *[1 mark]*.
(ii) Low rainfall means it will be hard for Egypt to produce a lot of food *[1 mark]*. This can lead to malnutrition and people who are malnourished have a low quality of life *[1 mark]*. People also have fewer crops to sell so they have less money to spend on goods and services *[1 mark]*. The government gets less money from taxes so there's less money for it to spend on developing the country *[1 mark]*.

Page 63 — Development and Aid

1 (a) (i) Bilateral *[1 mark]*.
(ii) Long-term aid helps the recipient country to become more developed *[1 mark]*. Also, the country will become less reliant on foreign aid over time *[1 mark]*. However, it can take a long while before the aid benefits the country, e.g. because schools and hospitals take a long time to build *[1 mark]*. Bilateral aid can also be tied, so the aid might not go as far as untied aid *[1 mark]*.
(b) Sustainable aid is aid that helps a country to develop in a way that doesn't irreversibly damage the environment *[1 mark]* or use up resources faster than they can be replaced *[1 mark]*. The aid described in Figure 4 is sustainable because it does not irreversibly damage the environment and doesn't use up resources except for money *[1 mark]*.
2 This question is level marked. There are also 3 extra marks available for spelling, punctuation and grammar. HINTS:
- *Make sure your spelling, punctuation and grammar is <u>consistently correct</u>, that your meaning is <u>clear</u> and that you use a range of geographical terms <u>correctly</u>.*
- *Start by giving some <u>background info</u> about the aid project, e.g. 'FARM-Africa is a non-governmental organisation that provides aid to eastern Africa. It was founded in 1985 to reduce rural poverty, and is funded by voluntary donations'.*
- *<u>Describe what's being done</u>, <u>how many people</u> it helps and <u>what problems</u> it solves, e.g. 'The Community Development Project FARM-Africa run in Semu Robi gives people loans to buy small water pumps to irrigate their farmland. This reduces the effects of drought in the area and helps around 4100 people'.*
- *<u>State</u> whether the project <u>is sustainable or not</u> and <u>explain why</u> it is or isn't, e.g. 'The Community Development Project is sustainable because it doesn't damage the environment or use up resources. Although if people use too much water there won't be enough left for people in the future and it will become unsustainable'.*

Section Eight — Industry
Page 64 — Types of Industry and Employment Structure

1 (a) Primary industry involves collecting raw materials, e.g. farming *[1 mark]*. Secondary industry involves turning a product into another product / manufacturing, e.g. making textiles *[1 mark]*. Tertiary industry involves providing a service, e.g. nursing *[1 mark]*. Quaternary industry involves scientists and researchers investigating and developing new products, e.g. in the electronics industry *[1 mark]*.

Section Eight — Industry

(b) (i) Many more people are employed in primary industry in Country B than in Country A *[1 mark]*. This is because in Country A machines have replaced workers *[1 mark]* and it's cheaper to import primary products from other countries *[1 mark]*.

(ii) Many more people are employed in tertiary and quaternary industries in Country A than in Country B *[1 mark]*. This is because Country A has a larger skilled and educated workforce *[1 mark]*, a higher demand for services like banks and shops *[1 mark]* and money to invest in the technology needed for quaternary industry *[1 mark]*.

(c) (i) 54° on pie chart (accept between 52° and 56°), so (54 ÷ 360) x 100 = 15% (accept between 14.4% and 15.6%) *[1 mark]*.

(ii) The percentage of people employed in secondary industry will initially increase *[1 mark]*. This is because as infrastructure improves, businesses will move their factories to Country B as labour is cheaper there *[1 mark]*. It will then decrease *[1 mark]* as Country B becomes more developed because it will be cheaper for businesses to move their factories to less developed countries *[1 mark]*.

Pages 65-66 — Location of Industry

1 (a) (i) Greenshire has nutrient-rich soil *[1 mark]*.

(ii) E.g. the orchard location could have been influenced by which area has a suitable climate for growing apples *[1 mark]* and good transport routes to deliver the apples *[1 mark]*.

(b) (i) Distance on map = 1 cm, scale is 2 cm: 1 km, so distance = 0.5 km *[1 mark]*.

(ii) It is close to the raw materials from the orchards *[1 mark]*, close to urban areas where there are lots of workers *[1 mark]*, and has good rail and road transport routes nearby *[1 mark]*.

2 (a) (i) 808442 *[1 mark]*.

(ii) E.g. the location is near an urban area, providing lots of customers *[1 mark]*. There are green open spaces nearby to provide a pleasant environment *[1 mark]*. There are good transport links, e.g. a train station nearby, so customers can get there easily *[1 mark]*.

(b) This is a good location for the company *[1 mark]*, because it is close to the university which will provide skilled and educated workers *[1 mark]*. It also has good transport links to allow workers to commute, e.g. main roads and a train station *[1 mark]*.

(c) This question is level marked. There are also 3 extra marks available for spelling, punctuation and grammar. HINTS:
- *Make sure your spelling, punctuation and grammar is <u>consistently correct</u>, that your meaning is <u>clear</u> and that you use a range of geographical terms <u>correctly</u>.*
- *<u>Describe</u> the different industries in your chosen country, with <u>at least two examples</u> for <u>each industry type</u>, e.g. 'Kenya has a lot of primary industry, such as the trona mine in Magadi and farms in the Western Provinces'.*
- *For each example you need to <u>explain</u> why that industry is located there, e.g. 'The Western Provinces receive enough rainfall to grow crops'.*

Page 67 — Location of Industry Over Time

1 (a) (i) In 2000 there is no longer any primary industry in the coal fields *[1 mark]*.

(ii) E.g. the coal fields could be exhausted so the industry has moved elsewhere *[1 mark]*.

(b) (i) There is no longer any secondary industry near to the coal fields *[1 mark]* or the city centre *[1 mark]*.

(ii) Environmental reason:
E.g. secondary industry is less reliant on coal as an energy source because it can use electricity from the national grid *[1 mark]*.
Social reason:
E.g. transport facilities may have improved so the work force can commute to areas outside of the city centre *[1 mark]*. / Changing government policies encourage industries to settle in different locations *[1 mark]*.

(c) E.g. changing capital investment patterns encourage industry to locate to new areas *[1 mark]*. / Improved road and rail networks and public transport allow the workforce to commute outside the city centre *[1 mark]*. / Improved transport allows customers to travel outside the city centre to shop *[1 mark]*.

Page 68 — Environmental Impacts of Industry

1 (a) (i) Fishing *[1 mark]*.

(ii) E.g. removing trees destroys habitats and food sources for animals and birds, reducing biodiversity *[1 mark]*. / Soil erosion is more common as there are fewer trees to hold the soil together *[1 mark]*. / Trees remove carbon dioxide from the atmosphere so cutting down trees increases carbon dioxide, which adds to global warming *[1 mark]*. / Trees help move water from the soil to the atmosphere. Without this, rainfall is reduced *[1 mark]*.

(b) E.g. mining — removes large areas of land, which destroys habitats *[1 mark]*, depletes water sources as it uses a lot of water *[1 mark]*, and can cause water pollution *[1 mark]*. / Farming — monoculture reduces biodiversity as there are fewer habitats *[1 mark]*, using pesticides can kill other insects *[1 mark]* and fertilisers can pollute rivers, killing fish *[1 mark]*.

2 (a) The factory would destroy wildlife habitats *[1 mark]*.

(b) The running of the factory could produce pollution, e.g. water pollution from textile dyes *[1 mark]*. It would also probably use energy from burning fossil fuels, which contributes to global warming *[1 mark]*.

Page 69 — Development and Environmental Impacts

1 (a) (i) One mark for graph completed correctly.

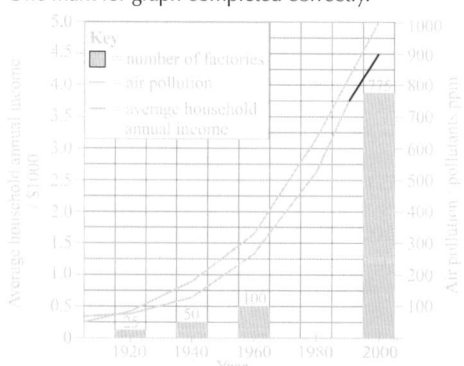

Section Eight — Industry

(ii) One mark for graph completed correctly.

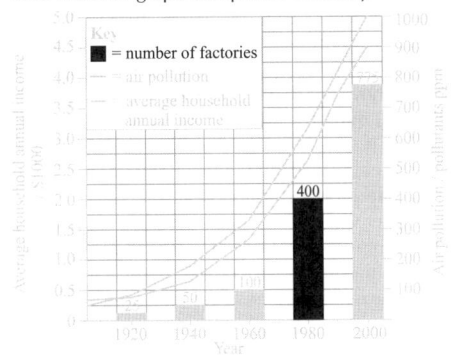

(b) (i) As the number of factories increased, so did the annual household income / there's a positive correlation between the number of factories and the annual household income *[1 mark]*. As industry grows, more jobs are created so annual income increases *[1 mark]*. As people earn more they spend more in the area and pay more tax so the economy of the area improves *[1 mark]*.

(ii) As the wealth of the area increased, so did air pollution *[1 mark]*. This is because there were more factories producing waste gases that pollute the air *[1 mark]*.

(c) E.g. introduce laws to reduce pollution *[1 mark]*. / Build factories on brownfield sites to stop habitat destruction *[1 mark]*. / Reduce energy use by using energy efficient technology *[1 mark]*.

(d) This question is level marked. There are also 3 extra marks available for spelling, punctuation and grammar. HINTS:
- Make sure your spelling, punctuation and grammar is <u>consistently correct</u>, that your meaning is <u>clear</u> and that you use a range of geographical terms <u>correctly</u>.
- <u>Describe</u> the <u>industrial activity</u> in your chosen location and explain how it has contributed to the economy, e.g. 'The Pearl River Delta in China has lots of large manufacturing companies...'.
- <u>Explain why</u> there's a <u>conflict</u> by describing the environmental impacts, e.g. 'There's a lot of air pollution in the area. Lots of it comes from power plants that burn coal. For example, the levels of sulfur dioxide in the air in the area are two to three times higher than...'.
- <u>Describe and explain</u> the strategies in place to reduce the environmental impact, e.g. 'The Government has pledged over US$7 billion to help clean up the Pearl River by building new sewage works and water treatment facilities'.

Page 70 — Global Climate Change — Causes

1 (a) Climate change is any change in the weather of an area over a long period *[1 mark]*.

(b) Global warming is the increase in global temperature over the last century *[1 mark]*.

(c) (i) 0.85 °C (accept 0.8-0.9 °C) *[1 mark]*

(ii) The temperature stayed between about 13.5 and 13.8 °C between 1860 and 1930 *[1 mark]*, and then rose fairly steadily to around 14.4 °C in 2000 *[1 mark]*.

(d) Greenhouse gases (e.g. carbon dioxide and methane) in the atmosphere trap outgoing heat *[1 mark]*, which helps to keep the Earth at the right temperature *[1 mark]*. This is called the greenhouse effect *[1 mark]*. Human activities like farming, forestry and manufacturing *[1 mark]* have increased the concentration of greenhouse gases in the atmosphere *[1 mark]*. This increase has caused global warming by making the greenhouse effect stronger *[1 mark]*.

Page 71 — Global Climate Change — Impacts

1 (a) E.g. habitats will be lost as low-lying coastal environments are submerged *[1 mark]*.

(b) 30 cm (accept 29 or 31 cm) *[1 mark]*.

(c) Rising temperatures and decreased rainfall will mean that some environments will turn into deserts *[1 mark]*. The distribution of some species may change due to climate change, and species that can't move may die out *[1 mark]*.

2 (a) (i) Rainfall has fluctuated but decreased from 1600 mm in 1985 to 1300 mm in 2005 *[1 mark]*. This has caused maize yields to decrease by around 30% between 1985 and 2005 *[1 mark]*.

(ii) Farmers' income may decrease if it becomes too dry for farming *[1 mark]*. Less food being grown could lead to malnutrition, ill health and death from starvation *[1 mark]*.

(b) E.g. climate change may cause people to move, which means some countries will have to cope with increased immigration and emigration *[1 mark]*. / Governments are under pressure to come up with ways to slow down climate change or reduce its effects *[1 mark]*.

Page 72 — Global Climate Change — Responses

1 (a) (i) They've agreed to monitor and cut greenhouse gas emissions *[1 mark]*. All countries have also agreed a target for how much they'll reduce their emissions by, e.g. the UK has agreed to reduce emissions by 12.5% by 2012 *[1 mark]*.

(ii) Countries that come under their emissions target get carbon credits that they can sell to countries that aren't meeting their emissions targets *[1 mark]*. This means there's a reward for having low emissions *[1 mark]*. Countries can also earn credits by helping poorer countries to reduce their emissions *[1 mark]*.

(iii) Some of the countries with the highest emissions haven't agreed to it, e.g. the USA *[1 mark]*.

(b) The tax rates are higher for cars with higher emissions *[1 mark]*. This encourages people across the country to buy cars with low emissions, so emissions are reduced *[1 mark]*.

(c) E.g. congestion charging is where local authorities charge people for driving cars into cities during busy periods *[1 mark]*. This encourages people to use their cars less, which reduces emissions *[1 mark]*. Local authorities can recycle more waste by building recycling plants and giving people recycling bins *[1 mark]*. Recycling materials means less energy is used making new materials, so emissions are reduced *[1 mark]*. Local authorities give money and advice to make homes more energy efficient, e.g. by improving insulation *[1 mark]*. This means people use less energy to heat their homes, so emissions are reduced because less energy needs to be produced *[1 mark]*.

Section Nine — Globalisation

Section Nine — Globalisation

Page 73 — Globalisation Basics

1 (a) It's the process of all the world's systems and cultures becoming more integrated *[1 mark]*.

(b) (i) One mark for line drawn correctly.

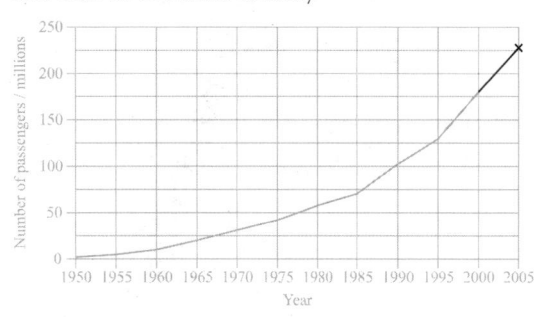

(Graph: Number of passengers / millions vs Year, 1950–2005, showing rising curve to ~230 million at 2005)

(ii) 170 million passengers (accept between 160 million and 180 million) *[1 mark]*.

(iii) It has made it quicker and easier for people all over the world to communicate face to face *[1 mark]*. It has also made it easier for companies to get supplies and distribute their products all over the world *[1 mark]*.

(c) MNCs are companies that produce products, sell products or are located in more than one country *[1 mark]*. MNCs increase globalisation by linking together countries through the production and sale of goods *[1 mark]*.

(d) E.g. improvements in ICT, e.g. e-mail, the internet and mobile phones, have increased globalisation *[1 mark]* because they make it quicker and easier for people all over the world to communicate with each other *[1 mark]*.

Pages 74-75 — Multinational Companies (MNCs)

1 (a) 15 *[1 mark]*

(b) (i) Mega Lomania's headquarters, research and development sites and most of its offices are located in MEDCs, e.g. in Europe *[1 mark]*. Most of Mega Lomania's factories are located in LEDCs, e.g. in Asia *[1 mark]*.

(ii) E.g. there are more skilled and educated people in MEDCs to work in offices *[1 mark]*. Labour is cheaper in LEDCs, which means Mega Lomania makes more profit by locating its factories in LEDCs *[1 mark]*.

(c) E.g. jobs will have been created *[1 mark]*. / Some skilled jobs, e.g. jobs in factory offices, may have been created *[1 mark]*. / Workers may get higher wages and a more reliable income compared to other jobs, e.g. farming *[1 mark]*. / Mega Lomania may spend money on infrastructure *[1 mark]*. / Mega Lomania will pay taxes that are used to develop the economy and country *[1 mark]*. / Local companies may supply Mega Lomania, increasing their income *[1 mark]*.

2 (a) (i) The jobs created aren't always secure as the MNC could relocate at any time *[1 mark]*. Profits go back to the country the MNC is originally from *[1 mark]*. Other local companies may struggle to find business so they shut down *[1 mark]*.

(ii) (160 million ÷ 100) × 5 = £8 million *[1 mark]*.

(b) E.g. if it's a large site it will attract lots of traffic, which increases pollution in the area *[1 mark]*. / The factory could produce pollution and waste, which is bad for the environment and for people's health *[1 mark]*.

(c) E.g. transporting raw materials (e.g. cotton) to factories and finished products (e.g. clothes) from factories increases greenhouse gas emissions *[1 mark]*. This adds to global warming *[1 mark]*.

3 This question is level marked. There are also 3 extra marks available for spelling, punctuation and grammar. HINTS:

- Make sure your spelling, punctuation and grammar is consistently correct, that your meaning is clear and that you use a range of geographical terms correctly.
- Start this answer by describing the MNC you've picked, e.g. 'The first Wal-Mart® store opened in 1962 in Arkansas, USA. Wal-Mart® now owns over 8000 stores and employs over 2 million people'.
- Next, describe the positive effects on the places that the MNC has located in, e.g. 'Wal-Mart® donates hundreds of millions of dollars to improve education, healthcare and the environment in the countries that it's based in. For example, it donated US $77 000 in 2008 to local projects in Argentina'.
- Then describe the negative effects the MNC has had on the places its located in, e.g. 'Some companies that supply Wal-Mart® have long working hours. For example Beximco in Bangladesh supplies clothing. Bangladesh has a maximum 60 hour working week, but some people claim employees at Beximco regularly work 80 hours a week'.
- Include as many specific details as you can.

Page 76 — The Impacts of Globalisation

1 (a) (i) The percentage of the total workforce in secondary industry fell from 50% in 1986 to 30% in 2006 *[1 mark]*. The percentage of the total workforce in tertiary industry increased from 15% in 1986 to 30% in 2006 *[1 mark]*. The percentage of the total workforce in quaternary industry increased from 5% in 1986 to 10% in 2006 *[1 mark]*.

(ii) E.g. it may have increased the gap between rich and poor people *[1 mark]* because people who have good qualifications can find work in tertiary and quaternary industries *[1 mark]* but poorer, unskilled workers would struggle to find work because there are fewer secondary industry jobs, e.g. in manufacturing *[1 mark]*.

2 (a) E.g. transporting raw materials and products around the world increases the amount of carbon dioxide released *[1 mark]*. This adds to global warming *[1 mark]*. / People have access to more products at low prices, so they can afford to be more wasteful *[1 mark]*. Lots of waste ends up as landfill if it's not recycled *[1 mark]*. / The more products that are transported around the world by ship, the more oil pollution there'll be *[1 mark]*. Oil pollution kills fish and seabirds *[1 mark]*.

(b) E.g. increased trade brings more jobs and money into the country. The government uses the money to improve infrastructure and services, e.g. healthcare *[1 mark]*. People have more money and access to lower priced goods so they can afford things like TVs *[1 mark]*.